*"This book will keep you three
steps ahead of the devil! Amazing
revelation of our victory!"*
—Sɪᴅ Rᴏᴛʜ, Host,
It's Supernatural!

JOHN RAMIREZ

EXPOSING
THE
ENEMY

**SIMPLE KEYS
TO DEFEATING THE
STRATEGIES OF SATAN**

DESTINY IMAGE® PUBLISHERS, INC.

P.O. Box 310, Shippensburg, PA 17257-0310

"Promoting Inspired Lives."

This book and all other Destiny Image and Destiny Image Fiction books are available at Christian bookstores and distributors worldwide.

Cover and interior design by Terry Clifton

For more information on foreign distributors, call 717-532-3040.

Reach us on the Internet: www.destinyimage.com.

ISBN 13 TP: 978-0-7684-5086-6

ISBN 13 eBook: 978-0-7684-5087-3

For Worldwide Distribution, Printed in the U.S.A.

1 2 3 4 5 6 7 8 / 24 23 22 21 20

"It's time to stop playing patty-cake with the devil and learn how to put hell on notice."

—JOHN RAMIREZ

Surely He shall deliver thee from the snare of the fowler, and from the noisome pestilence. Thou shalt tread upon the lion and adder: the young lion and the dragon shalt thou trample under feet.

PSALM 91:3,13

CONTENTS

A NOTE FROM
THE AUTHOR

I'm here on the ground with my nose in it since the whole thing began. I've nurtured every sensation man's been inspired to have. I cared about what he wanted and I never judged him. Why? Because I never rejected him. In spite of all his imperfections, I'm a fan of man! I'm a humanist. Maybe the last humanist. Who in their right mind, Kevin, could possibly deny the Twentieth Century was entirely mine?

Don't get too cocky, my boy. No matter how good you are, don't ever let them see you coming. That's the gaffe, my friend. You gotta keep yourself small. Innocuous.

Be the little guy. You know, the nerd...the leper...the sh*t-kickin' serf. Look at me: underestimated from day one. You'd never think I was a master of the universe, now would ya?

—AL PACINO,
portraying the character John Milton

If I didn't tell you who this character is supposed to be, and you just looked at the face value of this quote, you might think these statements are logical. Unfortunately, anyone falling for this type of logic is susceptible to Satan.

In the film *The Devil's Advocate* (Warner Bros., 1997), Keanu Reeves portrays Kevin Lomax, a Southern attorney with good morals, but an obsession with winning. John Milton invites Lomax to join Milton's law firm in New York, but then Milton puts Lomax in increasingly "grayer" legal scenarios where Lomax's moral judgment is compromised for wealth. Ultimately, these cases prove to be a test for Lomax as, at the end of the film, John Milton reveals himself to be Satan. As Milton so famously points out, "Vanity is my favorite sin; it is the gateway to all others."

While *The Devil's Advocate* is a work of fiction, imagine meeting a real-life Kevin Lomax, an individual who worked under Satan for many years and then finally pulled away and got a fresh start. Now imagine this person being willing to unmask Satan's tactics and offer both believers of Jesus Christ and the rest of the world the inside scoop on how Satan tries to lure humanity in—and why he has been so masterful at fooling billions of people over time. Imagine this person offering you the keys to defeat Satan's attacks and arming individuals with the tools they need to overcome Satan once and for all. Imagine no longer. My name is John Ramirez, and to quote the rapper Lil Wayne, "I've been to hell and back; I can show you vouchers."

Every word of my story is true and, what's more, it's a message that needs to be heard, now more than ever. People are eager to understand, not only the role of Satan in the modern world but how to combat him. The book you're holding will do just that. If you've ever doubted the power of Jesus Christ, even for a moment, after hearing my story I am hopeful you'll never do so again.

In my first book, I told the story of how I was trained to be the third-ranked high priest of a Satanic cult in New York City—casting power-ful witchcraft spells and controlling entire spiritual regions. But what started as a long spiral into the underworld ended, thankfully, in a miraculous encounter with Jesus Christ that changed the course of my life. I preach and speak from experi-ences that 99.9 percent of believers have never been exposed to. I've been in the enemy's camp, and I'm a defector.

People from all ethnic backgrounds dabble in the occult and fall victim to this Satanic under-world. Many of them think it is innocent and, trust me, it is anything but. People often get lured in because many of these cults claim to be based in part off of Christianity, or they promise answers on how to get closer to God. People get sent down a road where they lose themselves, fall under the influence of Satan, and never see the way out. With God's grace, I happen to be one of the rare individ-uals who made it out.

My hope is not only to help Christians learn how to expose and combat Satan, but to help those who are stuck find the pathway out. Within these pages, I share the teachings I have shared with thousands across the world to inspire them to live sanctified lives, fulfill their God-given destiny, and ensure that their soul spends eternity with God.

It's a message that needs to be told, and now more than ever.

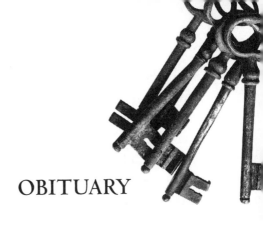

OBITUARY

DEAD MAN RAISED
TO NEW LIFE

New York, NY—On October 27, 1999 John Ramirez spiritually passed away late at night on his bed in the Bronx, New York. John was born in Puerto Rico and immigrated to the Bronx with his family as a child. He was the father of one daughter. John became the third-ranked devil worshiper in New York City in the spiritual realms of Santeria, Spiritualism, and Palo Mayombe. He was an evangelist for the dark side for twenty-five years and recruited many to "the religion." John enjoyed dominating the spiritual realm against Christians, the Church, and many other religions. In his Satanic mind, if he could control the region, he could control the people. He came conquering like his daddy, the devil: to kill, to steal, and to destroy many. But on the same night he "died" in the Bronx, he was born again—raised up a new creation in Christ Jesus—and armed with a new commission: to destroy the works of the devil and expose him, so that many souls could be set free.

CHAPTER ONE

THE CUNNING SERPENT

The greatest trick the devil ever pulled was to convince the world he didn't exist.[1]

The first thing you need to know about the spiritual being called Satan, or the devil, is that you won't find him running around in a red suit, with horns and a pitchfork. He won't come at you with bared fangs dripping blood. No! He would much rather you fall for the lie that he is just a myth and he doesn't exist at all. But if he can't convince you to swallow that, his next move will be to invade your life with all the hidden powers of hell, unseen but deadly.

When Jesus walked the earth, He warned us that the devil has a three-pronged mission: to kill, steal, and destroy. But then He added these precious words: "I have come that they may have life, and that they may have it more abundantly." Yes, the devil is real and very powerful, but there is someone more powerful than he: Jesus, the Son of God. If you don't know Him yet, my prayer is that by the end of this book you will.

In these pages I want to share with you how to uncover all the different ways the devil tries to invade your life. I will peel back the mask he's hiding behind and disclose his true nature, so you can be armed and ready when he comes. Together we will explore the reality of spiritual warfare and what it means to be a true soldier of the Cross. That's military language for good reason: you and I are in a war, an unseen spiritual war that reaches all around us, all the time. This is a war of darkness versus light, good versus evil. I should know; for twenty-five years I fought on the side of darkness, climbing the ranks of Santeria, Palo Mayombe, and spiritualism until I was the devil's number-three man in New York City, casting spells and plunging whole neighborhoods into Satan's grip.

You can read my testimony in the book *Out of the Devil's Cauldron*.

BIG DREAMS, LITTLE PEOPLE

I want to take you back for a moment to your younger years and mine. I remember in my first grade class one spring afternoon in early May, my teacher sat us down in a circle and asked us the ultimate question: "What do you want to be when you grow up?"

As I looked around the room in a panic, my heart racing a hundred miles an hour, I felt excited but afraid at the same time. Glancing around the classroom in a daze, with the big bright windows and bright yellow-painted walls, what stood out to me that moment was our finest artwork, displayed beautifully on the wall. Some of the artwork had little green hands, while others featured drawings of family faces or a few stick-figure family portraits.

As the teacher asked us this question, one by one, our emotions ran high. The excitement in the room was so thick you could almost cut it, as little people with big dreams yelled out "Me first; me first!" In the background I could hear some of my classmates yelling at the top of their lungs: "I want to be a police officer!" "I want to be an astronaut!" or "I want to be a fireman!" On the other side of the room another one yelled out, "I want to be a doctor!" Other classmates, their faces showing their confusion, didn't know what to say. Most of the girls agreed on being a nurse or a schoolteacher— or maybe even a ballerina. Surely, that was a fun day in class.

Nothing in our young hearts and minds was hoping and believing to become anything evil. Not even for a second , or a moment in time, did anyone yell out, "I want to be a murderer! I can't wait to grow up and be a serial killer or a drug dealer." Nor did any of the girls in the class raise their hands and say, "I want to be a prostitute and sell my body for money, or be in a bad relationship and later on get murdered." None of us that day had shattered dreams or false hopes.

As an ex-devil worshiper, I believe that the day you are born you start to die. You haven't yet said your first words, you haven't taken your first step, but as soon as you breathe your first breath, the devil has assigned a demon to chase after your life.

The thief comes only to steal and kill and destroy; I have come that they may have life, and have it to the full (John 10:10 NIV).

From the first breath you take, the devil and his demons' plans are to keep you away from the truth of knowing where you came from, away from knowing that you were designed to have a relationship with your creator, Jesus Christ, and away from knowing that at the end of the journey you are to return to where you came from: eternity with God. The plan of the enemy, whether you live in the penthouse or in the ghetto, is to distract every step of your life that was predestined by God to get you back home with Him. There was a discussion in Heaven before He gave you a birth date and sent you into time. *"Before I formed you in the womb I knew you, before you were born I set you apart; I appointed you as a prophet to the nations"* (Jer. 1:5 NIV).

THE MIND—SATAN'S BATTLEFIELD

Let me bring you into the enemy's kingdom and the strategy of the devil in a deeper way. The first thing the enemy attacks is your mind.

The enemy knows that the battle is in the mind, and he knows if he can capture the territory of your mind, your thoughts, and the way you operate, he's got you in a stranglehold. The next move he makes will be to attack your soul. This includes your mind, will, and emotions. Once he's got a person's soul, he will paralyze that person and bring them down to nothing. He has done this for centuries. He did it with Adam and Eve and with their son Cain, who murdered his brother, Abel. He did it with King Saul, who committed suicide, and with Judas Iscariot, who sold Jesus for thirty pieces of silver and later committed suicide.

> *And so, dear brothers and sisters, I plead with you to give your bodies [and minds] to God because of all He has done for you. Let them be a living and holy sacrifice— the kind He will find acceptable. This is truly the way to worship Him. Don't copy the behavior and customs of this world, but let God transform you into a new person by changing the way you think. Then you will learn to know God's will for you, which is good and pleasing and perfect* (Romans 12:1-2 NLT).

Doing this will keep you in the perfect will of God and out of the hands of the enemy, who wants to destroy your life. I believe that many Christians read the Word but never act on it, and the danger of this is that we leave ourselves open, unguarded, to the enemy's devices and entrapments and to the strongholds of the Satanic world. If we want to be more than conquerors, reading the Word is not enough. Acting on the Word and applying it—mixing it with faith—will destroy the enemy's game plan for your life.

The devil and his principalities (high-ranking evil spirits), who run the first and second heavens, and the junior "ground-level" demons, who operate on the earth today, have one mission—to capture your mind in a way that brings you to the point of no return. The enemy is clever; he studies each person—their character, their personality, their bad habits, their strong points and weaknesses. Then he sets traps based on all the information he has gathered, whether that person is a believer in Christ Jesus or not. He knows how to wait for the right opportunity to open the spirit realm in your life. This is how he gets that entry point into your life.

BABY STEPS TOWARD DESTRUCTION

For example, people like Charles Manson, Jeffrey Dahmer, Ted Bundy, and those who initiate mass shootings, and the beheadings in the Middle East all have one thing in common: they hear voices in their heads. The enemy has stolen their characters, their personalities, their will, and emotions because he was able to break them down to nothing and strip them of their identity. When I was a general in the devil's kingdom myself, I was taught these tactics of how to strip a person down to nothing and steal their identity.

The enemy knows how to set you up to take baby steps into the progression of your destruction. One of the most incredible psalms is Psalm 91. Look at what verses 3 and 13 say:

> *Surely He shall deliver thee from the snare of the fowler, and from the noisome pestilence. Thou shalt tread upon the lion and adder: the young lion and the dragon shalt thou trample under feet* (Psalm 91:3,13).

In these two Scriptures, the fowler represents the devil. I want to pinpoint his entrapments, which are the lion, the adder, the young lion, and the dragon. These are tools the enemy uses to set you up. The one that is most dangerous of all is the young lion. It is the setup that you don't see coming. This entrapment is smooth, under the radar, and it is the one opportunity described that you give the enemy to use against you. The young lion represents a "small" sin that you think you can control and put away whenever you want. For example, it could be watching porn movies or listening to dirty lyrics on a CD; it could be watching pornography on the Internet. It could also be smoking a marijuana cigarette once in a while.

Another example could be going to places that you know you shouldn't go as a believer. Let me give you the strongest warning someone could ever give you in your life. When you play around with or entertain a *"young lion,"* what you don't end up killing and putting away from you now will end up killing you: because when it's full-grown it becomes the lion or dragon that Psalm 91:13 describes. That's how the enemy gets his way to build strongholds in your life.

COMMON GATEWAYS AND PORTALS

Here are some other gateways and portals the enemy uses to keep you away from God's best.

Many of the things listed below are activities people engage in (even as children or teenagers) thinking they are just "innocent fun." I'm here to tell you, there's nothing innocent about them. Take part in any of the following and you are playing with fire—and propping the door wide open for the enemy's activity in your life:

- Mediums, psychics, fortune-tellers
- Tarot card readings
- Séances
- Horoscopes
- Paranormal phenomena
- Talking to the dead
- Seeking after ghosts
- Playing with Ouija boards
- Watching horror movies or television shows
- Listening to music with lyrics of profanity, murder, suicide, etc.
- Pornography

These are the devil's weapons of mass destruction that he uses against humanity without them even knowing it. Satan has a PhD in capturing your imagination. Once he has a hold of that, he then takes control of your life and owns it. In his timing, he will take your life out. He starts with your imagination and won't stop there. It will become a ripple effect into your family. Have you ever heard someone say, "My daddy was an alcoholic, and his daddy was too" or "So many people in my family tree committed suicide"? Why do you think there are so many generational curses, so much sickness, and so much destruction within families? That was never God's intent for our lives.

My warning as a watchman on the wall is this: stay away from these things!

THE DEVIL DOESN'T DISCRIMINATE

The devil doesn't work only in our normal lives or environment; he's after every piece of territory he can get. The devil's plan is that if he can take over the territory, he can control the people. He's out to claim territory, or spiritual regions, regardless of status—rich or poor, black or white, famous or obscure. I'll give you one example of this.

The devil goes to Hollywood. We watch television celebrities and movie stars and think they are sitting on top of the world. Some of us want to be them; we envy them; we even go so far as to imitate them and look like them. But if people in Hollywood could testify and speak the truth from their hearts, many of them would give anything to switch places with us. If you look deeply into Hollywood, you can see the face of the devil and how he has so many people in his pocket for a season.

These people shine like stars, but look again—the stars are falling. They suffer from depression, oppression, suicide, out-of-control lust, diseases, alcoholism, drug addiction; many are on so many prescription pills they can't keep track of them anymore. From famous singers to stars of the big screen and small screen (television), somehow, somewhere, they have made a pact with the devil. Some of the most famous Latino singers, for example, have reached the heights of success only to end up in a coffin, to be buried in a cemetery in the Bronx. If I were to name the name of one particular singer, you would know her songs. She sold her life to the occult "religion" called Santeria. Many others today are on the same route, on a train called "Hellbound," and the motorman also has a name:

his name is the devil. So the stars in Hollywood are falling.

THE DEVIL KNOWS YOUR NEIGHBORHOOD

Don't let these words scare you, but it's true: the enemy knows your neighborhood—and I don't mean in a Sesame Street type of way! Do you know your neighborhood as a believer in Christ? Demons are assigned to patrol and control your neighborhood: principalities, and junior demons taking orders from them. I want to give you a glimpse into the unseen demonic world. As an ex-demonic evangelist, I know the ins and outs of that world, how Satan strategically plants strongholds in our neighborhoods, and every day we walk by the strongholds and they become the norm to us.

Let me name a few of those strongholds in your neighborhood:

Mosques

A demonic place where the devil meets with his people, yet we pass by it every day and brush it off like it's nothing instead of laying hands on it, cursing it to the root, and removing it. These demonic temples are right in our territory where our families live and our children play.

Many people think Islam is an innocent religion. It is not. We are easily fooled because we see Muslims living their morals and staying faithful to the core of their religion, but what most people don't realize is that the "god" of Islam is a demon called Allah. These individuals are like sleeper agents until they are pressed to the point to defend their religion; then they manifest, and turn on you and on society.

At the carwash where I get my car serviced, 95 percent of the workers are Muslim. They are very kind and seem to be very genuine, but as soon as I start talking about Jesus Christ as the Son of God, or about radical Islam or the stuff on the news today, or how if a person leaves Islam they have a death sentence on their life and it shouldn't be that way—you should see their reaction. From acting nice and genuine, their features change and their body language changes and they start to manifest to another person.

Botanicas

The botanica is another place, another stronghold where people go to get tarot card readings and buy candles to do witchcraft with. Many people think that botanicas are just a part of the Spanish culture—no harm, no foul. They couldn't be more mistaken. These shops sell ingredients for the purposes of black magic. And when people get tarot card readings to make contact with dead relatives, what they don't realize is that the "relative" who shows up is a familiar spirit, a demon that mimics everything about the deceased person.

Liquor Stores

Liquor stores in our neighborhoods are breaking families up through a spirit of alcoholism. This spirit is destroying families, loved ones, friends, and entire neighborhoods, and we do nothing about it. When was the last time we prayed and took inventory of our own neighborhood and claimed it for Jesus Christ and believed God to turn it around?

Nightclubs

Whether they are Latin nightclubs playing Spanish music, or R&B, or rap music, or rock clubs, or techno clubs, it's all the devil's playground. The neighborhoods they are located in are under the control of spirits of lust, immorality, adultery, alcoholism, drugs, murder—the list is long. You may think you can go out for a night of dancing and innocent fun. Think again. When you head back home, those demons follow you to infiltrate your whole environment.

I believe the reason we are put in our neighborhood is to destroy the works of the devil. For that reason and that reason alone, God has given you a place to reside in that particular neighborhood. Many neighborhoods are under a curse of control by demonic forces, by spirits of murder, suicide, poverty, immorality, adultery, and homosexuality, by spirits of insanity that know how to steal your mind, spirits assigned to break up families, spirits of rape, molestation, and so on.

This warning goes out to Christians today. Many of us take it upon ourselves to move on our own understanding, either to another state, city, region, or borough (this can be like committing spiritual suicide). We so easily allow the enemy to relocate us. It doesn't matter if it's a high-end neighborhood or a low-income neighborhood; demons are assigned everywhere. We easily fall into the trap—the trap of the hands of the devil—and become victims instead of being victorious in Christ. We don't pray and seek the heart of God.

We don't fast anymore. We don't even inquire if it's God's perfect will for us to move geographically, when the devil may be setting us up to fall into his pit of destruction.

This does not only affect you, it affects your family too, chipping away at their purpose and destiny. You need to come to see that your purpose and destiny are also lined up with the region and the season you are in.

The number one danger for a Christian is to move out of God's timing. It is like trying to clap with one hand. Beware of the enemy's plan for your life. God has a plan and purpose for your life, but so does the enemy. *"Lest Satan should get an advantage of us: for we are not ignorant of his devices"* (2 Cor. 2:11).

It's so important for us to pray and hear from God before we make any moves, anywhere. The devil is looking for an opportunity to set us up. He knows the dangers of moving out of God's timing. He will seduce you with a better place, better school, and better opportunities. But remember: Just because something shines and looks good to us doesn't mean that God is in it. So be careful.

Pray before you take your next step. The devil knows how to place you in a neighborhood that you're not prepared for spiritually. The plan he is trying to accomplish is to dismantle you spiritually by placing you in one of his stronghold places, or a neighborhood that he controls. He does this to dismantle you and your family, to destroy or delay the plan that God has for your life.

One of the craziest things I've heard since being a Christian, and the thing that breaks my heart, is what comes out of the mouths of my brothers and sisters in the Lord when they're trying to move to another city or country. They say, "I wonder if there are any good schools there?" or "Are there any good shopping areas, or buses and trains close by?" I've never heard a Christian say, "I wonder if there's a Bible-believing church in the area that preaches the Word of God uncompromised." They are not concerned about their purpose or destiny in God, or the consequences of eternity. That's when you know the devil is setting you up.

WHO IS SEDUCING YOU?

I believe every person has two doors in their lives. One of the doors is your mind and the other is your heart. These areas are "gateways" into your soul. God and the devil are in a battle for the doors of your life.

"Behold, I stand at the door, and knock: if any man hear my voice, and open the door, I will come in to him, and will sup with him, and he with me" (Rev. 3:20). Who owns the doors in your life? Ask yourself this question, and be honest. I am offering you a "Get Out of Hell Free" card. I am asking you with an honest heart to reflect on this question: where do you want to spend eternity? I want to silence the voice of reasoning in your life. Sad to say, in many churches today, instead of listening to the voice of the Holy Spirit, people are captured and held hostage by the voice of their reasoning, which is the voice of the devil himself. He holds our minds and thoughts captive in such a way that brings circumstances and consequences to our Christian walk. This makes it difficult to "fight the good fight of faith" as believers in the Lord Jesus Christ.

When God gives us a test and we are taking the class, many Christians today, instead of getting an "A" and passing the test, end up with an "Incomplete" in life. It's like going to college and taking an expensive course, and somewhere in the middle we opt out and settle for an "Incomplete." A life that's lived in alignment with the Scriptures—a life of sold-out obedience to the Lord Jesus Christ—is the greatest defense against the evil one. Don't settle for an incomplete. Determine in your heart to go all the way with God, *"being confident of this, that He who began a good work in you will carry it on to completion until the day of Christ Jesus"* (Phil. 1:6 NIV).

In Chapter 3 we'll look at some more examples of these open doors in your life, which the apostle Paul called the fiery darts of the devil and his cronies. These are the entrapments they use to try to succeed over your life. But first I want to talk about his number one setup—that's the subject of the next Chapter.

SUMMARY

The craftiness of the devil has trapped fallen humanity—and all of modern society—in a gross lie. So many people are tied up in the hands of this creature called the devil, and they don't even realize it. From our earliest childhood to the end of our lives, if someone doesn't sound the trumpet and point to the Cross of Jesus Christ, we are doomed.

NOTE

1. A line made famous by the movie *The Usual Suspects* (Polygram Filmed Entertainment, 1995).

    The greatest trick the devil ever pulled
    was to convince the world he didn't exist.

CHAPTER TWO

IDENTITY THEFT—THE DEVIL'S FAVORITE GAME

Adam and Eve were created perfect by God, and the devil stole their identity. In the same way, the devil steals many believers' and unbelievers' identities by robbing and stripping them of who God created them to be.

The devil's ultimate purpose in his kingdom, with his demons and principalities, is to steal your identity. This tactic is designed to keep a person from the Cross, redemption, and salvation. It progresses from taking their purpose and identity to leaving that person just barely surviving.

Listen to these beautiful words of God to each of us:

> *Before I formed you in the womb I knew you; before you were born I sanctified you; I ordained you a prophet to the nations* (Jeremiah 1:5 NKJV).

"Before I formed you, I knew you"—that means that in eternity past you had a meeting with God. One of the reasons He was going to send you down to creation, through a birthday, through a place in time, was to fulfill an assignment. Yet somewhere in a hospital room (or wherever you were birthed), the devil assigned a demon to your life, to steal your identity.

Today we hear a lot about identity theft, which is when someone steals your social security number, your credit cards, and your bank accounts; we know that situation is a living hell. It can take months or even years to recover from the damages. Now imagine someone stealing your identity spiritually. This type of damage intertwines with your eternity and determines where you will end up. The devil has been doing this since the beginning of time.

Throughout the Bible we read of the lives of men like King Saul, Samson, Esau, Jonathan, and Judas; these are some of the names of people who allowed the enemy to get the best of them. If we were to discuss the names of people today whose lives the enemy has hijacked—people whose spiritual identities have been stolen—there would be millions of names.

The devil is trying his best to steal our identity and the identity of the Church itself. Following are some of the ways he operates, or tries to operate, in our lives, to take our identity.

MARRIAGES AND FAMILIES

In my past life as a devil worshiper, I was taught and trained to have no mercy in attacking the family through witchcraft to break their unity and separate them from one another, especially if they were married.

The devil hates human beings because we are made in the image of God; that's the one thing he hates most. The second thing he hates is the family. Those who work for his kingdom through witchcraft, the occult, and spiritualism (such as casting spells) are trained to destroy families because the family represents Christ in the Church. If you dismantle the family, you strip it from its true identity.

Let me share something very important here. The devil is OK with so-called families, or people who are involved in homosexuality: Men living with men and women living with women. When it was time to do witchcraft on them, we didn't have to dismantle the family at all because they were already in sin. To teach them a lesson when they crossed the line against us, we would attack their bodies with a spirit of infirmity so they would die; because their identity was already stolen.

WORKPLACE

Another place demons will attack to destroy and bring chaos to your life is through your workplace. If you are the man of the house—or the head of the home, as Christians call it—your identity is wrapped up in your ability to provide for your family. Wreaking havoc in this area will break and dismantle your finances, and divide and steal your home. The devil also frequently uses the workplace as a place of temptation to adultery and fornication, encouraging two people to form a "friendship" that escalates into full-blown immorality.

HEALTH

The devil will also seek after your health through addictions, drugs, alcohol, diseases, and sickness because he knows that your body was created to be the temple of the Holy Spirit (whether you're a believer or not). This is another way that he's an identity thief.

FINANCES

Your money is another area the devil will attack. Out-of-control finances will push you to create such a debt factor in your life that it often brings oppression, depression, anger, resentment, and even spirits of suicide into your life. As we know, many today couldn't carry that weight, and it has taken the lives of young and old, male and female, from all walks of life.

RELATIONSHIPS

Through abusive relationships, the devil steals your identity and your self-confidence. He releases a spirit of condemnation on you, a spirit of low self-esteem, and allows a spirit of torment to scorn your mind—to the point that you think nothing is left of yourself. He also uses improper relationships to introduce you to spirits of adultery and fornication, wrapping you so tight in a web of immorality that only the power of the Holy Spirit can break it.

These are many of the gateways that this monster called the devil uses to steal your identity. I have no respect for him whatsoever. He will take every opportunity to devour and eat away at your true identity.

> *Be sober, be vigilant; because your adversary the devil, as a roaring lion, walketh about, seeking whom he may devour: whom resist stedfast in the faith, knowing that the same afflictions are accomplished in your brethren that are in the world* (1 Peter 5:8-9).

I want to leave you with a thought. I heard this from a great preacher once. Please examine yourself on the basis of what I am about to share with you. If you have a dozen eggs and two break, how many are left? Would you then throw away the whole carton? The same is true of your life. Why would you quit and throw in the towel? Why would you turn away from God, and, if you're not a believer, why wouldn't you give God a chance? The point I am trying to convey to you is this: just because two circumstances of your life are not going the way you wanted, but ten circumstances are still good and healthy, why would you want to give up or give in to the enemy and throw your life away?

TEMPTATION AND DECEPTION: TWIN EVILS

The tools that the devil uses most often are temptation and deception. Temptation is to make you want to quit and give up on God, and deception is to make you believe that you're never going to come out of your circumstances. Satan has been plaguing the Church of Jesus Christ with these two lies since the beginning of time. But I encourage you, believer, not to fall into these traps. Examine yourself when the enemy is trying to afflict you with these two lies. Know that God is faithful, and look behind your shoulder, whether you've been saved one year, ten years, or twenty years; look at the footprints of Jesus behind you that have brought you up to this point, and see that God has never failed you. Hold on to that picture in your heart and mind through faith, and then you will not fall into the entrapments of this loser called the Adversary.

One of the greatest things the enemy does is to cause a person to make a permanent decision based on a temporary situation. I believe we get stuck on the broken parts of our lives and sit in those areas far too long, even though we know that storms don't last. It's time to get up from the ashes and dust ourselves off from the residue of life, look the enemy eye to eye, and take back our identity. In case you've lost it and can't find it, your identity starts at the Cross. Get back to that place, where everything begins and ends in Jesus Christ.

> *Therefore, if anyone is in Christ, he is a new creation; the old has gone, the new is here!* (2 Corinthians 5:17 NIV)

SUMMARY

How easy we make it for the devil to steal our identity. We are all born with a purpose for our lives from the hands of God—but then the fiery darts of temptation and deception invade our lives. I call them spiritual bombs, entrapments of the enemy, setups that take our very lives in a downward spiral from God's best, which He designed for us before the beginning of time.

CHAPTER THREE

SHUTTING OPEN DOORS

One of the biggest deceptions the enemy uses on believers today, and how he opens doors in their lives, is to convince them that they have their sin situation under control and can quit at any given time. This is the number one setup the devil uses to create strongholds in the life of a Christian.

Sometimes he hooks them into watching Internet pornography by placing little drops of temptation in their mind, or inflames an urge to discover pornographic movies. Sometimes he flashes images in the mind to captivate and seduce the person to their computer so they can fall into that trap. He plays on their emotions to open a gateway of the mind to have their body react a certain way that will leave the person with a sexual temptation to perform unnatural acts against their own body—acts that are against the will of God.

I have encountered Christians who have fallen into the filthy hands of the devil in these situations, and their minds have become so diluted that they confessed that performing pleasurable acts against their own body is not a sin. That is a lie from the pit of hell!

FALLING FOR THE LIE

The enemy will open portals, or doorways, to bring someone back to their past in their mind, before they were saved, especially if the person was delivered from certain strongholds such as drinking, drug addiction, or fornication, for example. He will use those old strongholds to tempt that person in order to bring them back to that place over and over. In a subtle, convincing way, the enemy will try to convince you that the grace of God will cover you and that it's OK to give into those temptations He has delivered you from. This is called premeditated sin. The grace of God should never be taken for granted.

In a similar way, if there was a season in our past in which we struggled with things such as unbelief, self-condemnation, shamefulness, abuse, or rejection, the demons will find ways—through our church, through other believers, or especially through family members—to bring us back to the ashes of these circumstances that the Lord has delivered or healed us from.

Another weapon that the enemy knows how to use is the negative words that come out of other people's mouths or—even worse—out of our own, to set up the trap that will drag us back into the mud. Our Christian walk shouldn't be that way. *"The tongue has the power of life and death, and those who love it will eat its fruit"* (Prov. 18:21 NIV).

HAPPY WORDS VS. TRUE FREEDOM

Many of the churches today (thank God not all) are "preaching us happy" but are never freeing us from the attacks of the enemy, from the pitfalls of life, and from the entrapments of the devil. These churches are not freeing us from broken marriages, from backsliders in our families, from bad soul ties, from generational curses that are never dealt with but are swept under the carpet, because the Church is not discipling us to receive the true freedom we have in the authority of Jesus Christ.

I have heard many times over from brothers and sisters in the Lord that they are led by the hand of demons into situations without realizing they are being set up. All you hear from these precious brothers and sisters is "I have a check in my spirit about that person," but they are not able to discern the danger that is ahead. Many times the devil sends people our way to destroy our destiny when God warns us to stay away.

DESTINY STEALERS

If we are caught unawares, we may miss God's warnings and fall into the enemy's hands and so create bad soul ties and bondages in our life. There is also another danger we seldom speak about that the enemy uses against us—it's the setup of being unequally yoked with unbelievers, or even marrying the wrong believer. Many times people have married another Christian that the Lord has not hand-selected for them: maybe because that person is not spiritually mature, or maybe there are things they haven't surrendered to the Lord, or maybe they are not connected spiritually to the ministry

God has called you for. They could also be a wolf in sheep's clothing, handpicked by the enemy to sabotage your ministry or your life.

The Bible is filled with stories we can learn from, about how to stay free from bondages and shackles that lead to bad soul ties. One of the saddest examples in the Old Testament has to do with Jonathan and King Saul, his father. When God gave this young man Jonathan a good soul tie, who was David, instead of cultivating that good soul tie, he kept his alliance and commitment to his dad. Jonathan felt obligated to go with his father all the way. I can only imagine if Jonathan had done a 180-degree turn and followed David. What would his life have been like? But because of that one bad soul tie, he came to an early death.

How can many Christians learn from this, including myself? These are strong warnings that we should never take lightly. The Lord has allowed these warnings to be in His Word for our own protection against the enemy. The devil knows our carnal desires better than we know ourselves. Many times he takes advantage when we give him those opportunities to create bad soul ties.

I say this with a sad heart, but many Christians today, because of the lust of the eyes and flesh and the pride of life, have made some bad decisions instead of agreeing with God. They came into agreement with the devil, and because of the consequences of their choices, they are not living God's best for their lives.

A DIVINE PARTNERSHIP

Do you know that you are in partnership with God? Do you know that there is a covenant made within this partnership? When you accepted Jesus in your life, you made an agreement to be in a partnership and you made a commitment to keep your end of the deal, to fight the good fight of faith (see 1 Tim. 6:12 and 2 Tim. 4:7).

The enemy is looking for every opportunity to distort, delay, and even to void your part of the contract. Many of my brothers and sisters today start strong, but somewhere down the line the demons get a hold of them and sabotage their part of their contract. Many have backslidden, and even have the audacity to say that Jesus didn't work for them. Truth be told, though, they never kept their end of the deal; Jesus works all the time, and all things work together for good for those who love Him.

Warning: who have you tied yourself to: the Cross or the world? The Bible says, *"Don't team up with those who are unbelievers. How can righteousness be a partner with wickedness? How can light live with darkness?"* (2 Cor. 6:14 NLT)

Let me leave you with this thought: Do you know the voice of God for your life? Or have you been listening to the voice of the devil?

SUMMARY

How easily we as believers, and especially nonbelievers, allow the devil and his henchmen to open doors in our lives, quick as lightning, but it takes a lifetime for us to close them. Be watchful in your walk with God. The devil is after us nonstop.

Many of us are so quick to believe the enemy of our lives over the eternal God, Jesus Christ, who created us—falling hard to the words we speak that are lifeless, that are hurting ourselves, hurting others, and grieving the heart of God.

If we are not vigilant, we may let our life slip away through the pitfalls of delay, believing distorted truth, generational curses, demonic friendships, and the people we connect to (bad soul ties), and so wind up missing God's best. The devil is relentless, but we have the victory in Jesus Christ. It's time to close those doors and never look back. Trust in the finished work of the Cross.

CHAPTER
FOUR

THE VOICE OF GOD AND
THE VOICE OF THE DEVIL

There are two roads in life, two directions, two voices, two paths, but only one journey, with signs and warnings ahead of us. If you had the opportunity to ponder your life today and look back and reflect on where you are standing, which highway of life would you enter and what signs were ahead? Which exits did you miss where you were supposed to get off? I believe that if you look hard enough into your journey, you will know that there are two voices trying to direct your path: the voice of God and the voice of the devil. Look at how different these two voices are.

GOD	DEVIL
Stills you	Torments you
Reassures you	Threatens you
Leads you	Pushes you
Enlightens you	Confuses you
Forgives you	Condemns you
Calms you	Stresses you
Encourages you	Discourages you
Comforts you	Worries you

The thief does not come except to steal, and to kill, and to destroy. I have come that they may have life, and that they may have it more abundantly (John 10:10 NKJV).

One voice leads to victory regardless of the potholes you encounter on the highways of life. Another voice comes to delay, steal, and alter the plans and purposes of your destiny and how it's supposed to play out in your lifetime. That other voice brings torment, sickness, confusion, fear, doubt, unbelief, letdowns, entrapments, delays, chaos, oppression, depression, suicide, even sometimes murder in the journey called life. That voice will steal your life away, regardless of who you are. It will give you the worst deck of cards that you could ever imagine and put you on the road to spiritual death, to the point of no return.

Caution: The Bible tells us that Satan can appear as an angel of light, and increasingly I see him using tactics to mimic the true Light—Jesus Christ—through New Age practices. Many times, people will fall into the trap of speaking to their "inner guide" or "spirit guide" or "ascended self." This garbage goes by a lot of different names, but the reality is that they're entertaining familiar spirits: Spirits who speak loving, self-affirming words to them and teach them "higher knowledge." My point is that you may hear sweet words and think, "this has to be God," because the devil likes to mimic everything God does, but with a perverted twist.

If a person continues on this path, the end result will be ugly. Eventually those spirits' true colors will show up, and the person's bondage will be complete. Anyone who practices "channeling" of spirit guides needs serious deliverance—a subject we'll get into later in this book. This is a form of witchcraft and demonic possession.

Don't be fooled, people. Ask God to help you discern good from evil. Holy angels do not have ongoing conversations with people; they may appear from time to time to deliver a message or encouraging word (we see this in the Bible), but if any "angel" tells you it's from God and wants to have a "walking/talking/guiding" relationship with you—it's a demonic spirit, pure and simple.

TWO VOICES IN A GARDEN

Let me take you back to the place where it all began—the voice of God comforted Adam and Eve in the Garden of Eden, where they had His sweet fellowship in their lives, day after day. But an interruption took place in the midst of the Garden, a second voice that was pure poison, and that voice came from the serpent, the devil himself, lying through his teeth. Here's a recap of the encounter that took place in the Garden of Eden:

> *But the serpent said to the woman, "You will not surely die. For God knows that*

when you eat of it your eyes will be opened, and you will be like God, knowing good and evil" (Genesis 3:4-5 ESV).

Prior to this conversation, God gave an order of trust, and told Adam and Eve that they could eat from any tree in the Garden except the Tree of the Knowledge of Good and Evil. I believe the reason God allowed this, and gave this order, was to give them freedom of will and build trust between God and man—which brings us into a pure relationship with God, based on those principles.

So here Adam and Eve had two trees, or really two opportunities to choose right from wrong; because if they disobeyed God's one command, He said they would surely die, which refers to spiritual death—and eventually results in physical death.

The devil, in his craftiness, seized the opportunity to turn man against God. How did he do this? By trickery of speech and by twisting God's words. That caused the Fall of man, and this has affected us down through the generations; until now, we think we have become like God, making our own decisions. Not only has the Fall decayed our lives and our families, but this entire world, by causing us to play God.

But in God's mercy, He spared Adam and Eve, by killing an animal in their place. This showed that someone innocent had to die on their behalf, which is a foreshadowing of the coming of the Messiah, Jesus Christ. Sin came into the world through Adam's sinful choice, but redemption was coming right after it. God already had a plan of salvation in motion. And today, as rebellious people, we have rejected that gift of redemption, and the devil laughs and is still conquering the opportunity for us to not only play God, but to keep spiritual death in humanity. Doors are also opened to demonic activity in the lives of those who reject God's way of salvation.

This is how spiritual warfare was born. God has given the Church the victory against the enemy and his kingdom. It's up to us to reinforce that victory.

WHICH VOICE WILL YOU CHOOSE?

Since that day in the Garden, down through the generations, many people have harkened to that voice of Satan. We have played a game to be God, thinking that we can be our own God, knowing right from wrong or good from evil. We have come down to nothing, a life of bad decisions, a life of emptiness and sorrow, but we don't have to stay there. I come to bring you good news; there is another voice—the one true Voice—and His name is King Jesus. He is the only way out from any nightmare you are facing today. It's time to turn to the Cross of Jesus Christ. Life is too short. *"Whereas you do not know what will happen tomorrow. For what is your life? It is even a vapor that appears for a little time and then vanishes away"* (James 4:14 NKJV).

Take a moment to examine yourself. You only have one life to live. If you knew you had only five years, ten years, twenty years, or even just days left of your life, what decisions would you make? Would you allow the devil to steal your life away? If you had one trip to make to the Post Office of Eternity and you asked the clerk for a change of address form, which address would you put on the form? Would it be Heaven or hell? Let's not even mention purgatory, as it doesn't exist.

In the Gospel of John during the crucifixion, there were two thieves on the cross; one repented and Jesus said to him, *"Today you will be with Me in Paradise,"* which means Heaven, not purgatory.

The other thief harkened to the wrong voice, and his outcome wasn't a pretty one, as he ended up in hell.

I leave you with this thought. I, John Ramirez, was given a second chance after twenty-five years of devil worshiping. If you are reading this chapter, this is your second chance. The God I know is a God of mercy, a God of grace, and a God of love.

This is your second chance. So please fill out this form and choose the way to your new home for eternity.

Change of Address Form:

First Name: Last Name:

Current Address:

Earth—Funeral Home of Your Choice:

Final Destination: Heaven or Hell?

Heaven is a place of peace, joy, love, mansions that go for miles, a place of no sickness or disease, no hurt, no torment, no pain, no tears, worship as you never heard on earth—a place where we won't ever say goodbye because no one ever dies, and the greatest joy is to be with Jesus.

Hell, which was created for the devil and his demons, is a place where you never see your loved ones again. It is a place of lowliness, torment, rejection, and despair—a place where your thoughts will remind you of how many times you rejected the free gift of salvation. In hell, souls are ripped apart by the tormentors, sorrow reigns forever, the smell of death (sulfur) pervades the atmosphere, and the only song you will ever hear is the wailing and screams of those who are there forever. There is no hope of ever escaping hell, because of the decisions that got you there.

> *For God so loved the world that He gave His only begotten Son, that whoever believes in Him should not perish but have everlasting life* (John 3:16 NKJV).

PRACTICAL SPIRITUAL COUNSEL FOR THE BELIEVER TODAY

Let's put hell on notice and be the victorious Christians that God called us to be. I want to educate believers and teach them how to stay free and out of the grips of the enemy. I would love to help many of my brothers and sisters who are not aware of spiritual warfare prayers. They depend on general prayers in their life to defeat the onslaught and the weapons of mass destruction that the devil has unleashed against the Church of Jesus Christ. General prayers don't work. The devil doesn't mind that we pray general prayers against the hellacious personal attacks in our lives. As a matter of fact, he loves it because they are ineffective.

Before we dive deeper into spiritual warfare in the upcoming chapters, let's go over a few things so you have a strategy for defeating the devil.

Step 1—Don't Fear: The first thing believers should do when under attack is fear not. Don't panic and don't let the devil put pressure on you in any attack or spiritual circumstance. As I mentioned in Chapter Two, one of the cleverest tactics the enemy uses is to get us to make a permanent decision based on a temporary situation. That clever deception costs us spiritual setbacks and delays in hearing from God. Always remember: storms don't last. The Word of the Lord says to be still and know that He is God (see Ps. 46:10).

For example, let's say the devil attacks you in the church you're going to. Somebody snubs you when you walk in the door, or a group of gossips starts talking about you. You get upset and angry, decide to take it personally, and leave the church. Rather than praying and seeking God for your best answer, you let the devil push you out of the church that God positioned you in for your spiritual growth. Now you run out from there to another church, spiritually disjointed because you made a decision in the flesh, and the devil uprooted you from the position of God's perfect will for you in that season and that place. You just made a permanent decision based on a temporary situation; now the devil's got you.

Step 2—Do Periodic Checkups: To avoid the gradual slide into sin and selfishness that plagues unwary believers, I recommend that you make an assessment every three months of where you are spiritually. Make an assessment of your relationship with Jesus and the season you find yourself in.

TRIAL, TEST, …OR OPEN DOOR?

One of the things we should ask ourselves when the devil releases his demonic agents against us is the following question: "Is this a trial or a test, or did I open a door to the enemy?" When we open doors to the enemy, we give the devil legal rights over that part of our life, creating strongholds that need to be broken.

Let me explain these steps further. A trial is a situation or circumstance that lasts for a long period of time, such as we read about in the book of Job. Historians say that Job's trial lasted a year. A trial could be many things, such as a financial setback, a marriage struggle, an illness or infirmity—such as when I went blind again in 2002, for no reason at all; it was an attack from the devil. That's when we have to make a decision: Either we trust God through the trial or we collapse.

A test is something that has a shorter season of attack, something we can go through in days or weeks, depending on how we handle ourselves in the battle. A test could be a bad day at work, or a weeklong series of bad situations, or small circumstances that frustrate, anger, or depress you. An example of a test would be falling out at work with a co-worker, or perhaps an unsaved family member offends you. How you react can either glorify God or open doors to the enemy. You know that you have passed the test when you either humble yourself and accept the situation, or you turn away from it and leave with peace in your heart, knowing you did what God expected you to do.

An open door is when we step out of the will of God and so give the devil a legal right to have the upper hand over us.

It is important to identify which of these you are confronting, so you can prepare for battle and trust God for your victory. If you're not sure, ask the Lord to reveal the answer to you, but usually there are distinguishing characteristics to each.

The snares of the devil could be watching unholy television shows and movies, because the devil is the prince of the air (he controls the media and has domain over it); what you speak out of your mouth, because the devil is after your words; or any gossip you entertain that comes in through your ears that contaminates your spirit man. Another very common open door that many Christians allow is being ensnared by the filth of pornography. The Bible makes it clear that you must guard your eye gate, ear gate, and mouth gate because these are portals that give the enemy legal rights to create strongholds in your life and entrapments that will damage your walk in the Light with the Lord Jesus Christ.

One of the things the devil doesn't want the believer to know is that the victory was already won at the Cross of Jesus Christ. All we have to do is reinforce that victory. It is sad to say that many of us, because we get caught up in looking at the circumstances of the battle in the natural, lose focus on that victory Jesus Christ has already won. We serve a supernatural God.

SUMMARY

You have a choice in this life—serve God or follow the devil. Two voices, two paths, but only one choice. I know it often doesn't seem that black and white, but it is. If we are not moving forward with God, taking territory for His Kingdom, then we have already made the choice to serve the one whom Scripture calls the enemy. Maybe you never consciously decided to serve either God or the devil. Trust me, many people haven't. But as the saying goes, "Failing to plan means planning to fail." In this case, failing to choose God—or to choose life (as Moses told the Israelites)—is the same as choosing to serve the evil one. Be sure you choose life!

EXPOSING JEZEBEL AND DELILAH SPIRITS— DESTROYERS OF THE CHURCH

PRINCIPALITY SPIRITS ON THE PROWL

I would like to start off by making it clear to everyone that the two demons discussed in this chapter will never be more powerful than our Lord Jesus Christ.

So we should ask ourselves, why are these two principalities—Jezebel and Delilah—bringing down churches today? That is a good and honest question, and I would like to shed some light on the reason why. Many of the churches today (thank God not all) are in bed with these two demons, one way or another. These churches are busy teaching and preaching Jesus, but they are not hearing Jesus teach them. My heart cries out even saying this, but many churches today are ichabod, meaning the glory of God has left the church. How sad for that to be said of any church today, and we are not even concerned about it.

Jezebel and Delilah are bringing down ministries of all sizes. Many megachurches have fallen and closed down because these spirits have infiltrated the house of God, and we don't even know how to cast them out and keep them out. We don't even realize they have come in until we see the aftermath of the destruction they leave behind.

Jezebel: Control and Murder

To understand the spirit of Jezebel, we must understand the genesis of this personality in the Bible. The first mention of Jezebel is the rebellion and manipulation done by the wife of King Ahab. It was actually this spirit operating through Queen Jezebel that caused the nation of Israel to turn away from God.

Jezebel carries a spirit of murder; Queen Jezebel killed over one hundred of God's prophets. It is no different in the times we are in today:—the Jezebel spirit is still killing (spiritually) God's leaders in the Church. Bear in mind that the spirit which produced Jezebel's existence, before its nickname was born, we refer to as a "she"; however this spirit is without gender. It can come through a female or male. It comes to kill, steal, and destroy. The number one objective and sign of a Jezebel spirit is that it comes as a controlling spirit but camouflages itself as a godly servant of the Lord.

In the days of old, this spirit dominated and controlled over 450 false prophets. This goes to show you the power that this spirit carries. This same demon is sitting in our churches today. Not only does this spirit captivate the pulpit and have our nation by the throat, it also operates through politicians, governments, mass media, literature, and entertainment. It controls the Internet, social media, radio, and television, through the filth of these channels of the airways. I am shedding light on this principality called Jezebel because my main focus is to expose her in the Church and teach the Church the signs that follow her, before she destroys your ministry and your life. This is my assignment from the Lord.

Delilah, Jezebel's Sidekick

There is another spirit that works side by side with Jezebel: the spirit of Delilah. This spirit has almost the same attributes as Jezebel, but is more subtle than a serpent and more cunning. It comes as a seducing spirit. It has seduced many of our leaders in our churches today and brought them down to nothing. To understand the spirit of Delilah, we must go back to the genesis of this personality in the Bible. The first mention of Delilah is in the book of Judges, chapter 16. This spirit is a fornicating, adulterous spirit, and it seduces a man or woman who is anointed by God to commit these acts in the church.

It is a spirit that knows how to vex you until it breaks you and steals your anointing. Like Jezebel, it strips your anointing and then kills the anointed person. It is sad, but you don't even know when it is happening. Look at the case of Samson, a man handpicked by God from birth who had an incredible anointing on his life. This anointing was his strength. However, he never heeded

God's warnings, and he ended up in the hands of this principality called Delilah. You know how the story ends, and it wasn't pretty.

The Jezebel and Delilah spirits flow largely unhindered throughout the Church today. These spirits flaunt themselves in our churches day and night, night and day, and across the world today, in the entertainment and fashion industries, in our schools and colleges. Where can you go in society that the influences of Jezebel and Delilah spirits are not felt? They are destroyers of our culture and society, and if we don't identify and remove these two principalities and know their attributes and how they infiltrate the house of God, how then can we help set the captives free in this world today?

Here are the twenty-one telltale traits of these two spirits for our ministries and our churches:

1. Bring fear (caused Elijah to run)

2. Attack ministers

3. Attack the anointing and those anointed

4. Only do their own will, never God's

5. Give the appearance of repentance, then they attack

6. Need to be praised, elevated; they worship themselves and get others to praise them

7. Have a possessive love to destroy and control

8. Are loyal until you disagree with them—then they rebel against you

9. Do all that is asked of them, as long as it is according to their overall plan

10. Plant seeds of discord in others that often lead to conflict or even division in a church

11. Use others to carry out their evil plans

12. Work alone; they only use others

13. Have their own agenda, never God's or other people's

14. Do not listen to God's voice or anyone else's

15. Are very religious: "I heard from God, and He spoke to me."

16. Seek positions of authority in order to control, discredit, and reach their goal

17. Are not committed to anyone

18. Seek affirmation and significance

19. Have illegitimate authority

20. Are convincing liars

21. Rebel when corrected

Warning: The goal of the Jezebel and/or Delilah spirit is to destroy leaders, ministries, and nations. So let's stop being a gentleman with the devil and his kingdom.

Everyone in the Church can learn to identify these two spirits. We pray against them, we fast, but we go into spiritual warfare the wrong way. That's why we can never get the victory in the battle. Without Jezebel there is no Ahab, and without Ahab there is no Jezebel. The devil knows this. For us as believers to win the war, we must discern the battle before we engage. Many times we engage but we never discern, and so we lose the fight. This doesn't mean that our God is not all-powerful—He is and always will be—but so many believers don't know how to discern the battle these days. How can we confront something when we don't know how to discern it? The devil knows that the Church is lacking in discernment and takes advantage of us. The apostle Paul warned us: *"lest Satan should get an advantage of us: for we are not ignorant of his devices"* (2 Cor. 2:11).

As a diversion, the devil gets our attention by having us focus too quickly on Jezebel or Delilah. The first spirit that attacks a church, long before Jezebel comes in, is the spirit of Ahab, over the church leadership. Why would Ahab come in before Jezebel? I'm glad you asked. The reason is that Ahab is the only spirit that can tolerate Jezebel, and that is a description of the leadership of today that is tolerating Jezebel in our churches.

The effect of this demon is to flood the soul of the leadership with weakness and fear. That's the nature of the Ahab spirit: to give his authority over to Jezebel. Another thing to note is that the Ahab spirit occupies areas of tolerance within the mind of the woman or man who is in leadership; this is most dangerous. This spirit operates the same way with the spirit of Delilah.

The spirit of Samson will take over the leadership before Delilah is ushered in. The attributes of a Samson spirit are anger, unforgiveness, control, and disobedience. When leaders operate under these conditions, this spirit has attacked them.

One of the testimonies I've heard is that Jezebel puts a black veil, so to speak, over the leadership's spiritual eyes so they won't see her coming. In order to gain power and authority over the leaders and anyone working there, the Jezebel spirit will manipulate herself into the hearts of the leadership and discredit those who are in her way, those who are working for that ministry.

Delilah, on the other hand, will seduce the leader of that ministry, or anyone close to the leader, into fornication or adultery. If these spirits are not discerned in time, they will destroy that ministry.

There are three "weapons of mass destruction" that the Church needs today, but which the Church has largely failed to recognize. With these weapons we can be constantly on the offense against the kingdom of darkness. The first weapon is a powerful intercessory team that has a spirit of unity attached to it. The second weapon is a team of spiritual warfare intercessors, and the third weapon is a team of deliverance ministers. We'll go deeper into these weapons in a later chapter.

SUMMARY

This is how we will win the battle, by identifying the patterns of these two demonic, so-called "sisters" of Satan's unholy kingdom, to bring them down to nothing.

CHAPTER SIX

THE DEVIL'S RELIGIONS

While we're on the subject of the devil's craftiness and deceit, you should know that he created the word religion. He established his kingdom through different religions, except Christianity—even though for two thousand-plus years he's tried to dilute or pollute it. Today, the enemy is in fact working through these other religions. This is another way he steals your identity.

I want to expose the devil for who he is through the religions he has established on the earth, as well as the demons in the spirit realm that are working behind the scenes.

ISLAM

First let's talk about Islam, a religion that calls itself a "religion of peace." During Ramadan, Muslims fast morning and evening for thirty days. They pray five times a day and attend their services in the mosque. The Koran, which was written by a murderous spirit, talks about infidels, and if you were to become a Muslim and then convert to a different religion, the Koran commands that you be murdered. Muslims torture their victims to the point of no return. They even take their own lives (which is a suicide spirit) in the name of Allah—who (in my opinion as a former Satan worshiper) is no god at all, but a demonic principality. In fact, in my former days I had a spiritual contract with the demonic principality named Zarabanda (an African name) that reigns over the Middle East. The favorite color of Zarabanda is green. If you go look at the mosque in Mecca, the most common color you see on their doors and flags is green. Then how is it that this religion of "peace" can get you to Heaven?

NEW AGE

How the devil has stolen the minds of those who practice this occult. He has brainwashed them into worshiping everything and anything that has been created and to believe in it with a counterfeit faith. What keeps them away from the truth? Why would they want to worship created things when they can worship the Creator who created those things? They have been hit by a delusional and delirious spirit, to think that putting their faith in created things and nature will get them to Heaven.

There is a demonic book out there that speaks half-truths (which is no truth at all). You can feel the demons jump off the pages when reading this book. Through these writings these demons can steal your identity and destiny.

Here is an example, from the book entitled *The Secret*. This is a book based on the Law of Attraction, which is said to determine the complete order of the universe and of our personal lives through the process of "like attracts like." The author claims that as we think and feel, a corresponding frequency is sent out into the universe that attracts back to us events and circumstances on that same frequency. For example, if you think angry thoughts and feel angry, it is claimed that you will attract back events and circumstances that cause you to feel more anger. Conversely, if you think and feel positively, you will attract back positive events and circumstances. Actually, feeling anger (in this example) only goes out to the spirit realm, and it gets the attention of the devil and demons, which gives them legal rights over your words and emotions, and all you bring back is an attack of hell on your life.

Proponents of this "law" claim that simply changing one's thoughts and feelings can attract desirable outcomes such as health, wealth, and happiness. For example, some people believe that using this "secret" can cure cancer. This is pure deception. The devil counterfeits the Kingdom of Jesus Christ and creates false healings by first afflicting the person with a disease and then removing it.

The book of Job shows how the enemy afflicted Job with painful boils from head to toe. Only the Lord was able to heal him, not the devil. But the devil tries to mimic God, as always, so what the devil does is afflict the person with a disease for a season and then stops afflicting them for another season. The person goes back to normal and calls this a healing, but it's no healing at all. This keeps them in demonic bondage with the enemy, as he now has legal rights to continue to afflict this person whenever he wants.

As Proverbs 18:21 states, *"The tongue has the power of life and death, and those who love it will eat its fruit."* The Bible says to speak life; the enemy uses the counterfeit by using the law of attraction to bring death. This is a counterfeit light like good karma or bad karma, which is demonic. One of the things I learned in the enemy's camp is that I had the power to attract people through their negative words. As God says in Deuteronomy 30:19:

> *Today I have given you the choice between life and death, between blessings and curses. Now I call on Heaven and earth to witness the choice you make. Oh, that you would choose life, so that you and your descendants might live!* (Deuteronomy 30:19 NLT)

SANTERIA

Santeria...what a joke. The word Santeria means the worship of saints. Right off the bat they are deceiving you and pointing the finger in the wrong direction, because the only one they should be worshiping is Jesus Christ. From the very beginning they are misleading you. There are no saints at all; they are demons. The foundation of their religion is based on five main gods, which they call Reachers. These are their names: Obatala, Yemaya, Ochun, Chango, and Oya.

These are five demonic principalities. They have given themselves these names, have deceived millions with their big deception because they infiltrate culture this way, and Santeria is one of the most powerful occult religions on the earth today. I lived that life for twenty-five years.

What a mockery this religion is; I despise Santeria. I love the people, but I hate the religion. They dress themselves in white for 365 days after their ceremony called Santo. They claim that dressing in white means purity. How is it that white clothes means purity? How do white clothes make the person pure? Purity should come from within the person, and the only way that can happen is through salvation through Jesus Christ. They also abstain from different types of food. How silly is this, because the demons told them so. The warnings, if you don't do this, are that you can pass away and be terminally ill and end up in the hospital. My question to them is, if the demon says stay away from drinking milk and eating eggs and rice or else you will die, but you have eaten eggs and rice and drunk milk for forty years and never died, explain this one?

These people are under a controlling spirit: a spirit of fear and torment. To make another point, these demons, the so-called Reachers, also force the people to stay away from wearing certain colors. For example, they can't wear a red, blue, yellow, or black dress, suit, T-shirt, or sweatshirt because something evil can happen to them if they do. How is it that from a child you have been wearing all these colors and nothing happened? Those that practice this religion should reflect on these facts and not be deceived. This is foolishness—God made all colors for us to enjoy!

CATHOLICISM

From my perspective as a former follower of Santeria (which is the worship of saints), Catholicism is the worship of the saints, which are idols, and the worship of Mary. How is it that you can confess your sins to man and your sins are forgiven, or pray to statues and they take your prayers to the Lord? How is it that saying three Hail Marys and three Our Fathers forgives our sins? How is it that praying the rosary gets you closer to God? What is this place called Purgatory, as the Scripture says in Second Corinthians 5:8: *"We are confident, I say, and willing rather to be absent from the body, and to be present with the Lord."* As well, Jesus told the thief on the Cross, in Luke 23:43: *"I assure you, today you will be with me in Paradise"* (NLT). Jesus said Paradise, not Purgatory.

SPIRITUALISM/PALO MAYOMBE

This is another joke; how they deceive their people. They throw these big demonic feasts where people get demon-possessed and the demons use their bodies to communicate with people in the feasts. They channel spirits—the so-called mediums—and these demons come down through their bodies. The first thing demons ask for is white or dark rum and a cigar. They smoke cigars and drink all night while possessing the people. And then the demons have the audacity to say to the same people that they shouldn't go to the bars, clubs, or any house parties or drink any kind of liquor because it's not good for them!

These demons even prohibit their followers from smoking cigars and cigarettes. What a lie. In the feast they can use you to do these things and it's OK, but not in your own leisure time. You are told not to because something bad can happen to you. This is deception. The only reason these demons do that is because they want your body to stay healthy so they can abuse you. I know this because I lived in that world for twenty-five years. They also use animals to "cleanse" you from your sins, which is another lie. The only person who can cleanse you from your sins is the Son of God. Santeria is a religion of lies. People are captivated by it like a whirlwind, and their life is controlled to the point that it doesn't belong to them anymore. How easy the enemy steals their identity.

TAROT CARDS

For the many people who like to get their tarot cards read, let me expose this deception, since I used to read tarot cards when I was in that world. Tea leaves and cups are the same thing. The readers operate the same way. They promise to tell you your future. They break the cards in three piles: past, present, and future. They tell you your past to amaze you, they tell you your present to captivate you. These readings are actually done by familiar spirits—demons that walk the earth, assigned to each person to become "familiar" with them. The Bible exposes them. Now these demons are going to tell you your future. They may say you will have a car accident, or they can see you getting a divorce, or they see one of your children is going to get sick, or they see how you're going to get a great job. Your response is, "My husband loves me" or "I love my husband," or "My family and children are healthy." The spirits will then say for you to wait and see, that these things are going to happen.

The devil doesn't know the future. But little do you know that the demon speaking through the card reader and telling you all these things is the demon you are taking home with you, and he will make all these things happen. Then out of desperation you will run back into the hands of the devil (through the spiritualist) and say, "Oh, everything you said to me happened!" The spiritualist will say to you, "I can fix those things for you and make them go away for a fee of $_____." Out of pure deception you will pay that fee, and the medium will call back the demon and your life will temporarily go back to normal. But you now have a demonic door opened in your life and the life of your family that the devil can walk in and out of anytime he wants. You have cursed your family down to the third and fourth generation as it says in Exodus 20:4:

> *You must not make for yourself an idol of any kind or an image of anything in the heavens or on the earth or in the sea. You must not bow down to them or worship them, for I, the Lord your God, am a jealous God who will not tolerate your affection for any other gods. I lay the sins of the parents upon their children; the entire family is affected—even children in the third and fourth generations of those who reject me* (NLT).

JEHOVAH'S WITNESSES

This is another avenue Satan uses to steal your life. They fabricated their own "Bible." They believe that Jesus is not the Son of God, but that he is a god. They don't believe in the Trinity or that the Holy Spirit is a person. They believe the Holy Spirit is like electricity—just power, but not a person of the trinity.

I know these things to be true because my mother was a Jehovah's Witness for eight years. I saw my mother get sick in a restaurant and be rushed to the hospital because she was allergic to seafood. Five times that evening she almost died. But the Lord Jesus Christ used that opportunity to reveal Himself to my mother that evening. I remember clearly that none of the Jehovah's Witnesses came to the hospital to pray for my mother. All the Christian believers rushed to my mother's side, knowing that she was a Jehovah's Witness. That evening the hospital room was undeniably filled with the presence of the Lord. And that night my mother gave her life to the Lord. She took back her identity that had been stolen for eight years. Thank God for Jesus Christ and His great mercy!

SUMMARY

These are some of the many religions the enemy uses to rob you from God's best in your life. Thank God that He has made a way through His Son Jesus Christ and you don't have to stay in bondage or shackles when you can be free.

CONCLUSION

Finally, let me share a revelation I got from the Lord on the importance of fighting back. If we start doing these things, we will see the victory of the Cross 100 percent. We have to reinforce that victory in the face of evil. Let's put the devil on notice. He picked the wrong house, he picked the wrong church, he picked the wrong family to mess with. But we are more determined than he is. Amen.

I would like to point out something quickly. As I mentioned above, Revelation 20:1-3 talks about the removal of the devil. Sweet; I love it!

Then I saw an angel coming down from heaven, holding the key of the abyss and a great chain in his hand. And he laid hold of the dragon, the serpent of old, who is the devil and Satan, and bound him for a thousand years; and he threw him into the abyss, and shut it and sealed it over him, so that he would not deceive the nations any longer, until the thousand years were completed; after these things he must be released for a short time (Revelation 20:1-3 NASB).

I love this part; I'll paraphrase it for you. The angel came down, grabbed the devil by the throat, threw him down into the pit, and chained him up. Please listen to this: He didn't come down with white gloves, like the Church is trying to fight the devil today. The angel threw him down because the devil is a nobody. This event is going to supernaturally change the world because Satan is supposed to be the prince of this world, or the god of this age; he's the god of the children of disobedience. He's the master of every occult group. This should be a wakeup call to all in the political world, the music world, and the entertainment world. Your time is short, just like your daddy's.

My prayers go out for all. It's time to open up your eyes and bend your knees to Jesus Christ. I say this for the sake of sav- ing your soul-man. I've been to hell, and I don't recommend it. I want to say that those who put their faith in Christ: Don't be deceived into thinking there's no spiritual battle taking place. Let's stop the lies about "we don't need to fight anymore against the kingdom of darkness."

Again, Revelation 20 tells it all. We have a war on our hands through the power of the Holy Spirit to defeat and destroy anything spiritual that opposes the Kingdom of our God. That is the mission that Jesus left on the earth for the Church to accomplish: To set the captives free.

OUT OF THE DEVIL'S CAULDRON

INTRODUCTION AND CHAPTER I

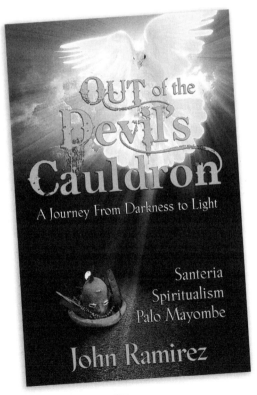

MARK OF THE BEAST

Shifting my feet to fight the cold, I waited at the busy crosswalk and watched my breath disperse like smoke in the wintry air. Though the temperature hovered in the low-20s, the main street through Castle Hill in the Bronx teemed with people as it always did this time of day. A cluster of little kids played at the curb, seemingly unaware of the traffic roaring past them just a few yards away. Someone leaned on their car horn and shouted obscenities at another driver. A police car zigzagged through traffic, its siren blaring and bleeping to make a path through the crush of vehicles. Home sweet home, I thought cynically. The light changed.

"Hey, John! What's happenin'?" a voice shouted.

I looked up to see a man I recognized from Step-In, the corner bar near the train station, leaning against the door of the barbershop. "Not much, man. Just keepin' it cool," I replied. We slapped hands in passing before I quickly turned the corner down a side street, not wanting to make small talk.

The cold wind whipping through Castle Hill hit me full in the face, and I turned up the collar of my wool coat. Though the winter chill invigorated me physically, something nagged at my mind—a troubled feeling I couldn't shake. I glanced up to see an older Hispanic woman outside her storefront staring at me, and as I turned my dark, piercing eyes on her, fear swept over her countenance. She made the sign of the cross and hurried inside, a bell jingling in her wake.

Go to your aunt's house. The same thought I'd had earlier that day came again, this time more insistent. By now it was unmistakable: the spirits were speaking to me. Go to your aunt's house. I considered not going, but only for a minute. Changing directions, I looped back the way I'd come but avoided the main street, arriving at Aunt Maria's three-story clapboard house within minutes. I rang the doorbell and waited, then rang it again. After the third ring I decided she must not be home, but something told me to go knock on the basement door. Stepping through the chain-link gate that accessed the basement entry, I started to knock when I saw that the door was already cracked open. I walked in.

Eerie vibes filled the room—vibes I knew well—and instantly I realized some sort of witchcraft ritual was in process. Through the dark I saw my aunt, a man, and another woman sitting at a mesa blanca, a "white table" used for witchcraft readings. I glanced at the floor in front of the table and saw strange symbols written in chalk with lighted candles on them, making it appear as if the floor were on fire. For the first time I got a good look at the man sitting behind the table. Short and stocky, he wore a bandana around his head like a biker, and his medium-length black hair was matched by coal-black eyes that seemed to pierce right through me. Whoever he was, I could tell he was in charge of this gathering, and his mysterious aura was strangely beckoning.

My aunt waved me over, not wanting to interrupt the reading. As the reading went on, I stared at the symbols on the floor, fascinated by the power and heaviness that hung like a lead cloak over the room. Witchcraft was no stranger to me—I had been casting spells and growing to new levels of power since I was ten years old—but the energy coming off this man was like nothing I'd ever felt before. Whatever it was, I wanted it too.

I listened as he described the different aspects of this religion until finally my curiosity won out.

"Hey, what's going on?" I whispered to Aunt Maria.

"This is Palo Mayombe," she replied in a monotone, tucking a strand of her salt-and-pepper hair back under her white bandana. As she said that, the man turned to me and opened his mouth to speak. My heart thumped like a jackhammer in my chest when I heard the words of his prophecy.

"This young man is your right hand and most faithful person in the occult," he said to my aunt. He held my eyes for a long moment, letting the words sink in. "He is a very powerful warlock who will become a major player in the religion. He must be in the first group of new initiates next month because of his power and commitment to Palo Mayombe."

Aunt Maria's eyes widened with awe, and I watched as a slow smile spread across her face. In that instant we both knew I had just walked into a supernatural appointment—her nephew was about to become a major power player, controlling spiritual regions of the Bronx.

That afternoon was a turning point for me. I knew I was going to another level in the spirit realm and would have power like I never knew before.

CONTRACT WITH THE DEVIL

The priesthood ceremony took place two weeks later in the basement of Aunt Maria's house. As I approached the house on foot, I could feel the rhythm of the conga drums vibrating on the night air. The sound of chanting inside told me that those who came to watch the ceremony—seasoned priests of the religion—were beckoning the spirits, setting the spiritual atmosphere for what would take place on that night in February 1997.

Opening the basement door ushered me into a world few people will ever experience. My aunt's basement had been transformed into a ritualistic chamber, dressed for a serious witchcraft ceremony. Flickering candles cast mysterious shadows on the walls, and seventeen tree branches covered the floor, one for each of the initiates to sit on. Two or three dozen roosters squawked from a makeshift cage in the corner of the room. I knew what they were for.

The music got louder and the songs more intense, with lyrics inviting the devil to come as the hours ticked toward midnight. Somebody asked the helpers to bring us into another part of the basement, and we stood shoulder to shoulder in front of what I sensed to be an altar. I felt the presence of demons so thick I could almost touch it. When the drumbeats reached their fullest a heavy presence beyond human comprehension descended on the room. Even though the words chanted were African and Spanish, I knew in my heart and soul and spirit they were summoning the devil.

It was Nafumbe, the devil himself.

Beads of sweat broke out on my forehead, and a strange mix of terror and excitement swelled within me. At five minutes to midnight, the high tata priest stood in front of me and started chanting some words, spelling out the contract that was about to take place. He chose me to go first. Taking a one-edged razor, he cut into my flesh. As my blood ran, I knew the contract was being initiated.

Out of the seventeen initiates that night, the devil chose only me to be initiated as tata, the calling of a high priest. The godfather cut a pentagram into the flesh of my right arm, distinguishing me from the others. The priests boasted about how seldom one is singled out for the calling of tata, and I held my head high: I had the mark of the beast on my body.

Early the next morning I woke up, bloody and swollen from the night's ritual, and made my way to the bathroom. It was still dark out and very quiet, but I could tell from the single small window in the basement that dawn would come soon. I flipped the switch to turn on the light and leaned in close to peer at my reflection in the mirror.

The face that stared back at me was the face of a new person, a new man. The black eyes that gazed from the reflection were eyes I had never seen before: I had been born into Palo Mayombe to be a Palero tata—a high priest.

CHAPTER ONE

BEGINNINGS

My blood boiling with rage, I walked into a bar and scanned the smoky room for my father, knowing he had to be here. Where else would he be when he was not at home or driving his gypsy cab? And there he was, just as I expected—sitting on a barstool, leaning in close to a woman with dark hair in a tight blouse. He was smiling and laughing, and I knew thoughts of my mother were far from his mind.

A movement across the room caught my eye. A man I'd never seen before glared at my father and clenched his fists. Even from this distance I could feel a thick vibe of jealousy and anger radiating from him.

The strange man reached inside his coat, and in that moment I realized what he was about to do— what I had secretly wanted somebody to do for a long time: kill my father.

Two shots rang out, and as my father slumped to the wooden floor, the stranger crossed the room to pump the rest of the bullets in the barrel into his cold, vile heart. While my dad lay dying, the bullet holes still smoking, I stepped from behind the stranger and stared down at my father's face. His eyes grew wide, and as his soul's silver cord was snapping I told him all he needed to do was show some love and concern for his wife and family. Just a little. Then his firstborn son would not have spent so many days and nights of his young life wishing his father was dead and finally seeing it come true.

The last words he heard me say were: "I wish it had been me who pulled the trigger instead."

The wail of a siren jarred me from sleep, and I sat bolt upright in bed, shaking in a cold sweat. A dream...it was only a dream. The same one I'd had over and over again since my father's murder the year I turned thirteen. I looked over at my brothers, snoring softly through the uproar of the South Bronx streets outside our dingy apartment window. The room was freezing as usual, but I was used to it. Unable to sleep, I crossed to the window and peered out. A couple of neighborhood thugs huddled over a trashcan fire on the corner, and a second police car roared down the street, its sirens chasing after the first one that had awakened me from the cruel dream.

How did I get here? I wondered. I was born in Puerto Rico but grew up in the Bronx as the oldest of four sons. From the Caribbean island of Puerto Rico, with its glorious sunshine, palm trees, warm breezes, and crystal waters, we moved to the harsh, cold streets of the South Bronx. As a child, I would fold my arms on an open windowsill on one of the upper floors of our apartment building and look out at the trash-cluttered sea of concrete, glass, and brick buildings. I had an artistic soul, even as a boy, but for miles into the horizon I saw no art or beauty. All I saw was an ocean of ugliness.

Good-hearted by nature, I was a spirited child who did my best to help my mother and brothers out. I knew my mother loved me, and that was very important, but what I craved most was my father's approval and love. It was something every growing boy needed. I longed for a dad to participate in my life, to say he was proud of me and that he loved me. It was something I never got.

Instead my absentee father had countless women on the side, bar fights, and drunken rages. His insane exploits ensnared him and saddened us deeply. I felt seething resentment even at a young age that he cheated us of a normal family's prosperity, blessings, and happiness.

His careless, cruel behavior toward my mother and our family became more horrible with each passing year. I would go from being a kind boy to being a very angry one. As time went on, my feelings and outlook on the world festered with the bitterness I felt. Eventually my once-kind heart turned stone cold.

THE BITTERSWEET BIG APPLE

My mother, Esther Martinez, was only a sweet sixteen-year-old when she married Eustaquio Ramirez in Santurce, Puerto Rico, and gave birth to me that same year in December 1963. The very next year she gave birth to my brother Julio. We stayed in Rio Piedras, Puerto Rico, for one year until my parents and both sides of their families came to the United States.

Upon arriving in America, in rapid succession my brothers George and Eustaquio Jr. came along. But the challenges grew deeper. As I got older I realized our family had not been prepared for the realities of living in New York.

This was supposed to be the start of a better life in the most promising city in the world—New York. Manhattan was the island that was so close, yet from where we lived in the South Bronx, it seemed a world away. It often felt like we were trapped in a time warp. We lived in an apartment prison with invisible bars that caged us in an endless, living nightmare.

The reality in which we lived seemed like a bad dream. My father, who was supposed to take the lead, instead was constantly running out of the home and out of our lives. He was missing in action for most of our lives. But when he did park the gypsy cab he drove for a living, we'd hear his keys jingle in the lock and he'd swing the front door open to step back into our lives. "Papi's home!" one of my younger brothers would yell. My dad was a young and handsome man with piercing eyes and thick black hair. Within seconds, bustling in her housedress and ever-present apron, my mother would put away any anger because of his absence, and her heart would be taken in again just by the sight of him.

He'd stroll into the kitchen for a bite to eat as though he had never left.

"What's the matter with these sons of mine?" he complained to my mom, pointing his finger at us as we stood in the doorway between the tiny living room and the cramped kitchen.

"They're good boys, Eustaquio. What do you mean?" my mother said, stirring a pot of yellow rice on the stove.

"If they were good boys they would ask for my blessing whenever they see me on the street like their cousins do," my father said. "'Bendicion, Tio!' they always say, but do my own sons ever ask me to bless them? No—all they ever want is a dollar so they can go buy candy." He glared in my direction, assuming that as the oldest I spoke for all four of us boys. Bitterness and hatred churned in my heart. I knew that a reply of any kind was useless. And then my father would make his way to the living room, fall out on the sofa in a drunken stupor, and go to sleep.

Often the next morning, although we were his own family, he seemed so detached, like his mind was elsewhere. It was as if he needed to be treated more like visiting royalty than a father, and we all tiptoed around and tried our best to please him and make him part of our lives.

My mother probably wanted to tell him news of her last few days or weeks. My brothers and I were bursting to share our baseball victories or basketball stories or talk about what happened in or after school. Maybe mention some cool car we saw or some girl we had a crush on, or even share a funny joke we heard. But more often than not we just ate in relative silence, afraid to say much of anything.

There seemed to be a gateless fence with barbed wire around him that we were afraid to scale, knowing we'd get cut. At other times it seemed more like a brick wall that we could never break through where he kept his emotions walled in, never expressing any real joy or love for us.

I never knew who my father really was and wondered if he even liked us, but I couldn't figure out why not. I saw other boys with their fathers going to the park, hitting a ball, playing catch, talking about sports. Those fathers would talk enthusiastically with them, pat them on the back, and walk along with their sons, sharing a good laugh. I yearned for that kind of relationship, but no matter what I tried he'd just push me away and call me "stupid." Some words are shattering to a child, and stupid is certainly one of them.

My father didn't seem to care that his dysfunction was so damaging. He seemed to go out of his way to discourage my brothers and me, to criticize us and talk to us in a condescending tone. We were never good enough to make him happy. And I swore I'd never be like him when I became a father and a man. I hated who he was, and I was even ashamed to tell others he was my dad.

Every now and then I held out hope that he would look at me and it would spark a glimmer of affection—in that moment he'd remember the little boy he once was. Or he'd want me to look up to him as the man I would one day become, but he left no positive impressions. The picture was either distorted or ugly or strangely blank. He left no template for me to pour myself into, no image for me to model myself after.

He frequently made promises, and like fools we let our hopes get high.

"Hey, John," he would call from the sofa, a beer in his hand. "This weekend, once my shift is over, I'll take you and your brothers to Coney Island. What do you say to that, huh?" His smile looked so genuine I believed him. "Want to go to the amusement park? Obey your mother all week and we'll go do the rides on Saturday."

But Saturday would come and my father was nowhere to be found. He had run out of our lives once again, to be missing for days or weeks on end.

Mom was the backbone of the family. With four children at a very young age, it was difficult for her to do things and move around from place to place. Since my mother was poorly educated and had no work experience outside the home, we depended on public assistance, food stamps, and whatever help my mother could get. Everything ran out after only a week or two, but we tried to make the best of it. From time to time my father would give her twenty dollars to buy food for the week. Even back then, that was not enough.

But at times it was much worse than that. Once I walked into the kitchen and stopped cold, staring in amazement at the five dollars he had left on the counter for food and other necessities. Five dollars! For his wife and family of four growing boys! Even with my grade school math I knew that five people (six whenever he came back home), divided by five dollars, meant my dad had left less than a dollar apiece for each of us to live on for the week. I also knew that even in the late '60s and early '70s that was no money. My mother used the basics— rice, beans, and potatoes—to stretch everything. But even with her creative and good cooking, five dollars was just a bad joke. What my father had left for us to survive on was more of an insult than a help.

"Five dollars! You know that's not enough to feed a family," my mother pleaded, her brow creased with worry lines.

"Then maybe you should put the five dollars in some water and stretch it," my father called back over his shoulder, a sneer on his face as he laughed at his joke. That was one of the many ways he humiliated my mother and controlled the family, by leaving us in lack.

WHERE ARE YOU, GOD?

Like so many others, my father was involved in espiritismo (spiritualism) and appealed to his gods in a darkened room with strange rituals, chanting, and candles. To him it was just a cultural thing. One afternoon toward dusk I walked down the hall of our apartment and heard my father chanting in the bedroom he shared with my mother. Tiptoeing to the door, I peeked through the crack and saw him before a makeshift altar glowing with candles. The sight of my father chanting to his favorite saint, whom he called San Lazaro (St. Lazarus), both frightened and fascinated me.

He often sent me with five dollars to the nearby botanica, a potion store, to buy an orange candle and flowers for San Lazaro, whom he probably loved more than his own kids. I could still hear his words throbbing in my mind: "Hurry and don't lose the money!" I would run down the stairs like a bat out of hell, trying to catch my breath and running past the people sitting on the front stoop. I was on a mission, dashing through cars in heavy traffic, my hands tightly gripped on the money. As I ran into the botanica, I hoped and prayed they would have what my dad sent me to buy. If they didn't, he would be disappointed—and angry with me.

Unlike many other Hispanic families, my family never went to the big Catholic church in our neighborhood, but I had seen the crucifixes and pictures of Jesus and heard people call Him "God." If He was God, why didn't He show up in my life? Why did He allow my brothers and me to hurt at the hands of our own father—not to mention the anguish my mother endured? I pushed the thoughts aside as quickly as they came. It was too painful to dwell on what the answer might be.

One afternoon I went down the block to play in the schoolyard, but to my surprise I heard loud music emanating from it. Curious to see what all the commotion was about, I drew nearer and saw a large red tent with a church service going on underneath. Somebody was playing a keyboard, and a choir swayed at the back of the tent as they belted out songs about Jesus. For a while I stood at a distance, touched by the music and stirred up in my heart. I couldn't put my finger on it, but instinctively I knew something very special was going on in this place. While the choir sang, a man came around off the stage and touched people on the forehead randomly. Whenever he touched them, they fell to the ground onto their backs, as if going to sleep. They looked so peaceful lying there, and suddenly I wanted the same thing to happen to me. I felt a love there that was indescribable.

As if on cue, the man leading the event started moving in my direction. My pulse quickened. One by one he touched people in the crowd near me, the closest one being a man standing right next to me. The man fell out on his back, and I could see the blessing on him—that something special I longed for too. I looked up expectantly, waiting for the minister to touch me, but he had passed me by, moving to another section of the crowd instead. I left that event feeling heartbroken, unwanted, and unloved. Why couldn't it be me they prayed for? Why couldn't it be me they touched? The answer that flickered through my mind: I guess God doesn't love me either.

MY FATHER, MY ENEMY

Most nights my father came home already roaring drunk and enflamed by rage. For no reason at all, or any feeble excuse, he would beat my mother. My brothers and I cowered in our rooms, trembling with fear. We were all just little boys, and I would bite my lip and beg God to make the screaming and hitting stop.

One night the sound of my mother screaming pulled me out of a deep sleep. I leaped from the top bunk bed where I slept and stumbled down the hallway, my stomach churning in knots. As I approached the kitchen, the sound of shattering glass exploded in the air. My dad had come home drunk—at two o'clock in the morning—and demanded the meal my mother always had waiting for him.

"You good-for-nothing woman! I don't know why I put up with you!" he yelled, looking for something else to throw. My mother sobbed as she tried to serve him the dinner she spent all afternoon cooking. Suddenly a reheated meal of beans, rice, tomatoes, chicken, and plantains went airborne as he slammed his dinner plate against the wall.

"Eustaquio, nooo!" my mother wailed. I watched my father's face—her reaction flipped a switch in his drunken brain and unleashed a monster.

He grabbed her by the hair and began to beat her mercilessly. At one point during his pounding, my mother—literally knocked out of her shoes by him—managed to break away and run barefoot in terror down the hall into their bedroom. She struggled to lock the door in a futile effort to escape him. He lunged after her and broke down the door, and her screams grew louder as the beating continued. Though I was still a young boy, I knew I had to rescue her. I bolted into the room and jumped on my dad's back to stop him from hurting my mother. He turned around, eyes blazing with fire, cursed me, and tore me off him with rough hands, throwing me violently across the room. I hit the floor hard in a broken heap, feeling physically and emotionally hurt, angry, and powerless as he continued to beat my mother.

Finally, at four o'clock in the morning, his rage spent, my father passed out and the house returned to its now-eerie quiet. Shaking with fear and anger, I crawled back into my bunk bed and tried to go to sleep. In just three hours I would have to wake up, get dressed, and go to school as if nothing had happened. I would have to show a brave face to the world, pretending that my home life was not the living hell it truly was.

That night as I examined my bruises and thought about the injuries my mother must have too, my hatred for my father grew stronger. It was that night I first wished my father was dead. I didn't realize it then, but one day my wish would come true.

A PLAYBOOK TO THE ENEMY'S TACTICS...

While much of the Church sleeps, dark forces from the underworld are being unleashed with increasing violence and perversion. Yet God stands prepared to display His awesome deliverance and transforming power through a remnant of Christ-followers who know they are called to kick in the gates of hell.

John Ramirez is living proof that you can go to hell and back. A former high priest of a New York-based satanic cult, he wreaked havoc on unsuspecting people for years before he had a supernatural encounter with Jesus Christ and broke free from Satan's kingdom.

Unmasking the Devil is an eye-opening primer that provides firsthand accounts of how Satan's army works. John teaches believers how to arm themselves with the power of the Holy Spirit to destroy the works of darkness in their lives.

John Ramirez is a watchman on the wall for such a time as this. In his first book, *Out of the Devil's Cauldron*, he told the chilling story of how he was groomed to be a high-ranking priest in Santeria, spiritualism, and the occult.

John's passion for setting people free continues in *Unmasking the Devil: Spiritual Warfare—Patterns and Cycles of the Underworld*. Within these pages he exposes the works of darkness on a greater level, giving believers a "playbook" to the enemy's game tactics.

> *"Spiritual warfare is a must for every Christian if they are going to survive in the coming years,"* says John Ramirez. *"It's time to stop playing patty-cake with the devil and learn how to put hell on notice."*

ABOUT THE AUTHOR

John Ramirez is an international evangelist, author, and speaker. For sixteen years he has been teaching believers from the Virgin Islands to Germany and on TV shows such as *The 700 Club, TBN, The Word Network,* and *The Church Channel* how to defeat the enemy. If you are interested in having John speak at your church or appear on one of your media shows, contact him at www.JohnRamirez.org.